Student
DISCUSSION GUIDE

to

Nothing But the Truth

By Nancy Romero

Talent Development Secondary
Center for Social Organization of Schools
Johns Hopkins University
Baltimore

© 2014 by The Johns Hopkins University, All Rights Reserved
These materials were developed by the Talent Development Secondary Program of
The Center for Social Organization of Schools
Reproductions without permission are prohibited.
Cover photo: http://www.flickr.com/photos/62693815@N03/6277209256/ Creative Commons CC-BY-S.A. 2.0

Discussion Guide #1

Pages 1-70

Vocabulary List A

designated (p. 1)
appropriate (adj., p. 1)
*reluctantly (p. 5)
capacity (p. 5)
*potential (p. 5)
facilitate (p. 11)
*contemporary (p. 18)
entice (p. 18)
vital (p. 18)
beneficiaries (p. 18)
municipal (p. 20)
*controversial (p. 21)
electorate (p. 21)
allocated (p. 25)

The Writer's Craft

Structure

The **structure** of *Nothing But the Truth* is unique. The structure of a novel is the way its different parts (such as characters, plot, setting, and form) come together to create a unified story. Many novels are told in narrative or "storytelling" form, from the point of view of a narrator who is outside of the story. However, there are other ways to tell a story. You have probably read novels written from the point of view of one of the characters in the story (the *first person point of view*). Other novels take the form of *journal or diary entries*. Still others are told through letters that the characters exchange (these are called *epistolary novels*). Some novels are written in the form of poems, while others take the form of a script similar to the script of a play; still others include "official reports" of the events in the story.

The structure of *Nothing But the Truth* is unusual because it includes a number of different forms and points of view. As you read the following chapters, note the different forms the narrative takes. What form is noticeably *not* included? Also, note the changes in point of view. How is the structure of this novel unlike others you have read? In what different ways does the author communicate the characters' actions, emotions, and thoughts? Do you think this is an effective way to communicate these things?

DISCUSSION QUESTIONS AND ACTIVITIES

Section I. Read pages 1-39. Discuss your responses to the questions and activities with a classmate. Then write your answers separately.

1. **In the left-hand column of the T-chart below, list things Miss Narwin has said about Philip's character and personality. In the right-hand column, list things Philip has said about Miss Narwin's character and personality. After completing your chart, tell which things listed are true about the character being described and which are not. Cite examples from the novel to support your opinions.**

Miss Narwin's View of Philip	Philip's View of Miss Narwin

2. **Describe the unusual structure of this novel. Why might the author have used this structure for *Nothing But the Truth*? Do you like the structure? Why or why not?**

3. How does Philip respond to his poor grade in English and the fact that as a result he is barred from trying out for track? How does Miss Narwin respond when she is not given funding for the teaching course she would like to take? How are their reactions to these situations similar?

4. In these first chapters, lack of clear communication has caused some of the problems described. List at least three incidents where lack of communication caused a problem.

5. **Explain how Philip has been dishonest with his parents about his situation at school. Why does he lie? Predict what problems might occur later because of his dishonesty.**

6. **What *rights* and *responsibilities* does Philip have in addressing the problem of his English grade? What *rights* and *responsibilities* does Miss Narwin have in this situation? Are either of them fulfilling their responsibilities? Explain.**

Make A Prediction:

Will Philip and Miss Narwin learn to work out their differences? Or, will Philip find a way to transfer out of her class?
Will Philip's dishonesty continue? Predict a future conflict in the story.

Vocabulary List B

*leisurely (adj., p. 55)   *vigilant (p. 55)   insolence (p. 60)
bedlam (p. 55)   stamina (p. 55)   infractions (p. 63)

 ### The Writer's Craft

Irony

Irony is present when a character's statements or views contradict what actually exists. Instead of telling the reader about the contradiction, the author allows the reader to discover it in the text of the story. As you read the following section, observe which statements and perceptions are not consistent with what is really happening. How is the title of the novel ironic?

DISCUSSION QUESTIONS AND ACTIVITIES

Section II. Read pages 40-70. Discuss your responses to the questions and activities with a classmate. Then write your answers separately.

1. **Do you think Miss Narwin is overreacting to the "Star-Spangled Banner" incidents? Why or why not? Do you think Dr. Palleni handles the situation well? Why or why not?**

2. **How are Mr. Malloy's words inconsistent with his actions? How are he and Philip alike?**

3. How is Dr. Doane's encouragement of Miss Narwin similar to Mr. Malloy's words of support to Philip? How do both Dr. Doane and Mr. Malloy fail to help Miss Narwin and Philip?

4. These chapters contain more examples of dishonesty, twisting of the truth, and careless reporting of facts. Identify three incidents in these chapters in which a character has not been completely truthful in his/her statements.

5. *Foreshadowing* is the literary technique in which clues are given about events yet to occur in the story. What is being foreshadowed about the "Star-Spangled Banner" incident? How is it being foreshadowed?

_____
_____
_____
_____
_____
_____
_____
_____

Make A Prediction:

**Will Philip accomplish his goals?
Will any of the characters confess his/her dishonesty?
Predict how one character will change in the course of the novel.**

 ## Literature-Related Writing

1. Write a **letter** to Miss Narwin giving her advice on how to improve relationships with her more difficult students.

2. Write a **letter** to Philip giving him advice on how to improve his English grade and earn the right to try out for the track team.

3. Write **morning announcements** for your school in a format similar to the one used at Harrison High. Also, create Mr. Lunser-type jokes to be added between the lines of the announcements. Read the announcements (and the jokes) for your classmates.

 ## Extension Activities

1. With one or more classmates, act out one of the scenes in the first eleven chapters of *Nothing But the Truth*.

2. Make a drawing of the one of the characters in the novel.

3. Create a poster of homeroom rules for your class.

Discussion Guide #2

Pages 71-142

Vocabulary List A

provocative (p. 76) *obscure (p. 89) *condone (p. 100)
infraction (p. 83) *arbitrary (p. 96)

 ### The Writer's Craft

Humor

An author who writes a story with a **humorous** tone hopes readers will be entertained by the funny characters and situations he or she has created in the novel. Some authors create ridiculous characters and plots that are not realistic. Others create stories that contain realistic humor. Which kind of humor does this novel contain? Which scene do you consider the most humorous so far?

STUDENT GUIDE 11
Pages 71-142

DISCUSSION QUESTIONS AND ACTIVITIES

Section I. Read pages 71-103. Discuss your responses to the questions and activities with a classmate. Then write your answers separately.

1. **Why isn't Philip willing to apologize to Mrs. Narwin and avoid suspension?**

   _____
   _____
   _____
   _____
   _____
   _____
   _____
   _____

2. **In the callouts below, write what each character would have stated as the reason for Philip's suspension. Could any of these characters have brought an end to the conflict? Explain your answer on the next page.**

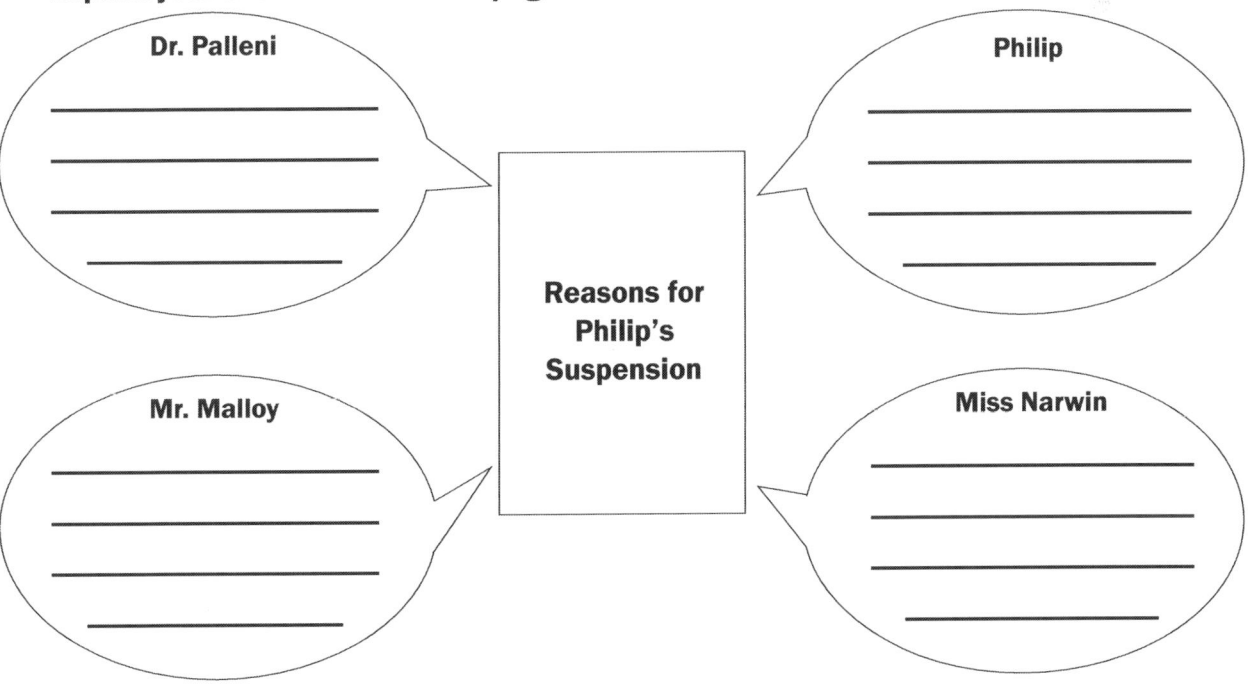

Talent Development Secondary Program

3. How is Ted Griffen using the "Star-Spangled Banner" incident to his own advantage?

4. In the middle column of the table below, identify the responsibility of each character listed in dealing with this situation. In the right-hand column, indicate whether or not the character acts responsibly, and explain your thinking.

Character's Name	Character's Responsibility	Does This Character Act Responsibly? Why or Why Not?
Miss Narwin		
Philip		
Dr. Palleni		
Mr. Malloy		
Ted Griffen		
Ms. Stewart		

Make A Prediction:

Will Jennifer Stewart get a clearer understanding of Philip's story when she calls the school? What will her news article say about the incident?

Who will lose the most as a result of the news article? Who will gain the most?

Vocabulary List B

*confidential (p. 107)   elemental (p. 125)   commotion (p. 140)
generation (p. 125)

 ### The Writer's Craft

Satire

Nothing But the Truth is an example of **satire**. Satire is a type of literature that ridicules human faults. It is usually written to inspire improvements in society. Satire may be gentle and sympathetic in its criticisms or biting and angry. Which kind of satire is used here? What human faults has the author ridiculed in the previous chapters? As you read the following section, notice the satire. What needed improvements in society does it suggest?

DISCUSSION QUESTIONS AND ACTIVITIES

Section II. Read pages 104-142. Discuss your responses to the questions and activities with a classmate. Then write your answers separately.

1. **What is the author satirizing in this section of the novel?**

2. **Is the news article an accurate summary of the information the news reporter received? Is it a true account of what occurred? Explain your answer.**

3. Is the media always motivated to report the facts of a story as accurately as possible? Why or why not? What happens when only one side of a story is presented?

4. Does any character in the story have a totally correct view of what occurred in the classroom between Miss Narwin and Philip? Explain your answer.

5. What does Dr. Seymour mean when he says, "... it doesn't matter whether it's true or not true... it's what people are saying that's important"?

_____
_____
_____
_____
_____
_____
_____

Make A Prediction:

In Philip's diary entry dated March 31 (page 117) he considers the possibility of asking Miss Narwin for extra work so that he can get on the track team. Do you think he will carry through on this idea? Why or why not?

As the novel goes on, will any character change his or her view of Philip's suspension? Will any character regret his or her inaccurate reporting of the events?

How will the national news attention affect Philip and Miss Narwin?

Talent Development Secondary Program

 **Literature-Related Writing**

1. Write an **article** about an incident or issue in your school or community. Try to present an unbiased account by researching the point of view of various individuals or groups involved. Submit your article to a school or community newspaper for publication.

2. Read an article in a local newspaper about a topic that interests you. Read critically and attempt to identify any words that show an attempt to slant the story. Also, notice how the author states the facts of the incident or issue. Do you sense that important information is missing? Does the article raise unanswered questions? Has the writer been fair and clear in his/her writing? Write a **letter to the editor** telling whether or not you think the article was fair. Provide evidence to support your opinion.

3. Who or what do you think is most to blame for the problems that have occurred since the incident at Harrison High? Write your opinion along with supporting reasons in a brief **essay**.

4. Write a brief **skit** that satirizes (pokes fun at) an irresponsible, unkind, or unfair behavior that is common at your school. (Remember, the target of your skit should not be specific individuals, but a behavior that is common to many in the school community.)

 **Extension Activities**

1. Tell two brief stories about yourself to your classmates. One should be true and the other false. Be sure to make the false story believable. See how many classmates can identify the true story.

2. With other students, perform the satirical skit that you wrote for Literature-Related Writing option #4.

3. Select one of the irresponsible behaviors that *Nothing But the Truth* criticizes. Create a poster that encourages people to correct this failing.

Talent Development Secondary Program

STUDENT GUIDE
Pages 143-212

Discussion Guide #3

Pages 143-212

Vocabulary List A

raucous (p. 143)
*emphatically (p. 151)
random (p. 155)
indicative (p. 155)
animosity (p. 155)
inferior (p. 155)
option (p. 155)
misconstrue (p. 177)
*prohibits (p. 179)
monitor (v., p. 179)

DISCUSSION QUESTIONS AND ACTIVITIES

Section I. Read pages 143-180. Discuss your responses to the questions and activities with a classmate. Then write your answers separately.

1. **How does Allison's account of the "Star-Spangled Banner" incident differ from Cynthia's? Does either account support the statement that Philip sang the national anthem "in a loud, raucous manner"? Explain your answer.**

Talent Development Secondary Program

2. **Dr. Doane and Dr. Seymour both change the memo written by Dr. Palleni on the "Star-Spangled Banner" incident to make it more convincing and better suited to their own purposes. In the chart below, list at least three changes that Dr. Doane makes to Dr. Palleni's memo and three changes made by Dr. Seymour to Dr. Doane's memo. In the right-hand side of the chart, list reasons why the changes were made.**

Changes Made by Dr. Doane	Reasons for Dr. Doane's Changes
Changes Made by Dr. Seymour	Reasons for Dr. Seymour's Changes

3. **How does Ted Griffen use the incident at the school in his speeches to urge listeners to hold down the cost of education? Is his argument a good one? Why or why not?**

4. How do Philip's parents expect him to feel about the letters and telegrams he has received? How does he really feel? Why do you think he feels this way?

5. Why is Philip anxious about returning to school? What is ironic about his statement to Ken Barchet about track and Mrs. Narwin's English class?

STUDENT GUIDE
Pages 143-212

Make A Prediction:

Will Mrs. Narwin keep her teaching job?

Will Philip be able to smooth things over with his classmates? Will he resolve his conflict with Miss Narwin and earn the opportunity to try out for the track team?

Will Ted Griffen be elected to the school board? Will the school budget pass?

Vocabulary List B

tenure (p. 187)
expedite (p. 194)
sabbatical (p. 194)
*rational (p. 198)

*equitable (p. 198)
compromises (p. 198)
prudent (p. 198)
fiscally (p. 198)

*resign (p. 200)
petition (p. 203)
*candid (p. 209)

 **The Writer's Craft**

Theme

A **theme** is the major idea or message in a work of literature. The theme may be clearly stated in the text of the novel or it may be implied ("read between the lines"). A theme often presents a broad truth about people, society, or the human condition. A novel often has more than one theme. What theme(s) have you recognized in *Nothing But the Truth*? Was the theme implied or clearly stated? As you read the last section of the novel, decide how the story's theme is expressed in its conclusion.

Talent Development Secondary Program

DISCUSSION QUESTIONS AND ACTIVITIES

Section II. Read pages 181-212. Discuss your responses to the questions and activities with a classmate. Then write your answers separately.

1. **What deal does Dr. Seymour make with Ted Griffen (pages 184-187 and 198)? What does each hope to gain from the deal? Are they successful? Explain your answer.**

2. **How have both Miss Narwin and Philip changed since the beginning of the story? How have they remained the same? Do you have sympathy for either character? Why or why not?**

3. Explain the irony of Philip's first day at Washington Academy.

4. How are Miss Narwin's and Philip's decisions at the end of the book similar? What is *ironic* about each of their decisions?

5. **The story does not end well for either Miss Narwin or Philip Malloy. Why did the author choose this ending for his story? What theme(s) do you see in this novel?**

_____
_____
_____
_____
_____
_____
_____
_____

 ### Literature-Related Writing

1. Write a **letter** to either Philip or Miss Narwin to encourage him or her to return to Harrison High. Suggest things that this person might do to improve his or her experience for the next school year.

2. Design a **poster** entitled, "How to Communicate Well and Avoid Misunderstandings." Write a list of ten things to do or avoid based on what you have learned in *Nothing But the Truth*.

3. Write a **diary entry** Philip might write after his first day of school at Washington Academy.

 ### Extension Activities

1. With a classmate, act out one of the dialogues in this section of the novel.

2. Draw a cartoon that expresses one of the themes of this novel.

3. Make a collage that expresses a theme of this novel.

 **ABOUT THE AUTHOR**

Avi, whose full name is Avi Wortis, was born in New York City in 1937. He grew up in a politically active family of artists, musicians, and writers. As a boy he had great difficulty writing, and this problem, later recognized as a learning disability called dysgraphia, caused him to struggle in school. Avi's family placed great emphasis on books and reading, and, in spite of his dysgraphia, he determined while in high school to become a writer. He started his career as a librarian and has published children's novels since 1970. His novels have won many awards and are written in a variety of genres. Avi's stories are popular because they are fast-paced, action-filled, imaginative, and often humorous. The stories are at the same time thought-provoking, often commenting on American culture, and feature endings without full resolution. Other works by Avi include *The True Confessions of Charlotte Doyle*, *Night Journeys*, *The Man Who Was Poe*, and *The Escape from Home*.

 SO, YOU WANT TO READ MORE

If you enjoyed reading *Nothing But the Truth,* you might enjoy reading other novels that show high school characters in conflict with school administrations and policies, such as Perry Nodelman's *Behaving Bradley*, Margaret Yang's *Locked Out: A Novel*, and Robert Cormier's *The Chocolate War*.

Made in the USA
Lexington, KY
28 October 2016